KT-450-767

Queen
Victoria

Susanna Davidson

Designed by Karen Tomlins

History consultant: Dr. Kim Reynolds

Reading consultant: Alison Kelly
University of Roehampton

Queen Victoria's Family Tree

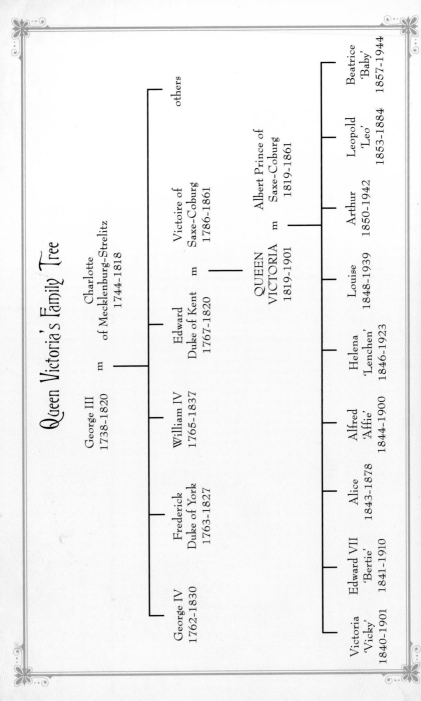

George III
1738-1820

m

Charlotte
of Mecklenburg-Strelitz
1744-1818

George IV
1762-1830

Frederick
Duke of York
1763-1827

William IV
1765-1837

Edward
Duke of Kent
1767-1820

m

Victoire of
Saxe-Coburg
1786-1861

others

QUEEN
VICTORIA
1819-1901

m

Albert Prince of
Saxe-Coburg
1819-1861

Victoria
'Vicky'
1840-1901

Edward VII
'Bertie'
1841-1910

Alice
1843-1878

Alfred
'Affie'
1844-1900

Helena
'Lenchen'
1846-1923

Louise
1848-1939

Arthur
1850-1942

Leopold
'Leo'
1853-1884

Beatrice
'Baby'
1857-1944

Contents

Crowds waving to Queen Victoria on her coronation day.

Chapter 1

The little princess

The young princess, small and sturdy with huge blue eyes, looked angelic. But she didn't act it.

"You must do your piano practice like everyone else," said her teacher.

"No!" shouted Princess Victoria, banging down the lid of the piano. "There! There is no *must* about it."

By the age of five, the little princess had developed a fearsome temper and a powerful will of her own. All her life, she had been pampered and worshipped by the two women closest to her – her nurse, Mrs. Brock, and Baroness Späth, her mother's lady-in-waiting.

But she had a new governess now, Louise Lehzen, who was determined to transform the tyrant toddler into a well-behaved princess. Lehzen described Victoria as the most "passionate and naughty child" she had ever met.

A portrait of Victoria from 1823, when
the princess was four years old

Once, refusing to learn her lessons, Victoria had
gone so far as to hurl a pair of scissors at her.

But Victoria soon grew to adore Lehzen, who
realized the way to Victoria's heart was to be
affectionate but firm. For thirteen years, Lehzen
never left her side. Victoria was, as she later
wrote, "her only object and her only thought."

A young Princess Victoria with her
mother, Victoire, the Duchess of Kent

Although Victoria was a princess, her family
was far from rich. Her father, the Duke of
Kent, was the King's fourth son. He had lived
extravagantly and died in debt when Victoria
was only eight months old. Her mother
Victoire, a German princess, had been left
alone in England with no money and no friends,
unable to speak the language. She longed to
return to Germany, but her brother, Leopold,

persuaded her to stay in England and bring up her daughter as an English princess. After all, he argued, not one of the King's first three sons had produced a surviving heir. There was a chance that Victoria could one day be Queen.

So Victoire, known as the Duchess of Kent, set up home in Kensington Palace, with the baby princess and Princess Feodora, her daughter from her first marriage. There they lived in a grand but sparse apartment. The rooms were shabby and cold. The wind wailed around the chimneys and the damp carpets were threadbare and crawling with beetles.

This is the East Front of Kensington Palace, as it looked in Victoria's lifetime. Victoria and her family lived in an apartment on the ground floor.

Even after five years in England, the Duchess still felt friendless and alone. She missed her son, Prince Charles of Leiningen, away at school in Geneva, and was terrified that the King or his brothers would take Victoria away from her, to be brought up at Court. For help, she turned to John Conroy, a dashing Irishman who had worked for her husband.

A portrait of John Conroy, painted in 1830, when he was forty-four years old

Handsome and scheming, with a family of his own to support, Conroy used all the charm he possessed to take control of the Duchess's life. If Victoria came to the throne before her eighteenth birthday, he realized, her mother could be appointed Regent, to rule in her place. And if he controlled the mother, then he would be the power behind the throne.

Together, the Duchess and Conroy came up with a plan known as the 'Kensington System', to make Victoria popular with the British people. But there was a more sinister side to their scheme. Worried that one of Victoria's uncles would claim the Regency, they wanted to separate Victoria from her father's family. They also wanted to make sure the Duchess had such a strong influence over her daughter that the country would *have* to make her Regent.

As Conroy's control increased, Victoria's life began to change. She was rarely allowed to play with other children her own age. She was closely watched at all times, and when she went to bed, Lehzen remained on guard until the Duchess came to bed. Then mother and daughter slept in the same room.

Even though Feodora was twelve years older than Victoria, in the stifling atmosphere at the palace the two became very close. Many years later, Feodora recalled how, "My only happy time was going or driving out with you and Lehzen; then I could speak or look as I liked."

Victoria longed for friends, to visit her uncles and be part of the excitement of court life. Instead, she poured her affection onto her governess, describing her as, "precious Lehzen, the best and truest of friends." She also turned to the make-believe world of dolls. Together, Lehzen and the princess would spend hours playing with the dolls and making elaborate costumes for them out of velvet and silk.

Here are four dolls from Victoria's collection. She had 130 in all, and gave each one a name, some after real people, others imaginary.

Then, in 1828, Feodora left home. Conroy had arranged her marriage to a poor German prince, wanting to send her away so she couldn't persuade Victoria to rebel. Princess Feodora was desperate to get away too. "I escaped some years of imprisonment which you, my poor dear Sister, had to endure after I was married," she wrote later.

Victoria missed her sister terribly, writing to her constantly, sending news of her dolls and even writing letters from them. "I was delighted to see a little letter from you directed to me from your darling hands," Feodora wrote in April. "How often I should like to kiss them and your whole little person."

As Victoria's sense of isolation deepened, Conroy felt his plan was finally falling into place. In January 1827, the Duke of York died, leaving Victoria second in line to the throne. Conroy even persuaded the King to give him a Knighthood.

Victoria was given finer clothes – layers of velvet and lace, thick sashes and puffy dresses, and was also allowed down in the evening to greet her mother's guests.

Her lessons changed too, becoming more rigorous and demanding. Her mother employed a string of tutors to teach her writing, geography, arithmetic, scripture, English, Latin, French and German. On Thursday she had a dancing lesson and on Friday, music.

Victoria was growing up to be disciplined and hard-working, but she still played with her dolls, needing her make-believe games to whisk her away to another time and place. And she still had problems with her temper. Lehzen began to keep a book noting down Victoria's tantrums. Victoria often confessed to having them three days in a row, although afterwards she was always filled with remorse.

When Victoria was ten, her mother invited the Bishops of London and Lincoln to inspect her, to make sure her education was fit for a princess. Their only suggestion was that Victoria should learn how likely it was that she would be Queen. Lehzen slipped a family tree into her history book, and for the first time, Victoria realized how close she was to the throne. "I cried much on learning it," she later said, and prayed she would never have to be Queen.

An artist's impression of Princess Victoria
discovering that she is likely to inherit the throne

Conroy was determined not to leave anything
to chance. In 1830 he began to suspect that
Baroness Späth, the Duchess's lady-in-waiting,
was spying on him for the King. He soon
convinced the Duchess, who had her fired.
Victoria was devastated, fearing that her mother
was going to send Lehzen away too.

Princess Victoria, in 1833, with her beloved pet spaniel, Dash

Members of the royal family were also worried about Conroy, writing to the Duchess to tell her that he had too much influence over her. But the Duchess refused to listen.

In June 1830, George IV died and the Duke of Clarence became King William IV. At sixty-five, he was the oldest man yet to become King. Conroy and the Duchess decided to take a tour of the country, to boost Victoria's popularity and show her off as the heir to the throne. The Duchess also wanted the people to see her at her daughter's side. They were met by waving crowds wherever they went. The Duchess loved it, but Victoria felt isolated and alone. She had only Conroy's daughter for company and she missed her home and her pets. For the Duchess, it was a triumph. On her return, Parliament promised that she would be Regent if Victoria came to the throne before the age of eighteen.

The older Victoria grew, the more the Duchess watched and controlled her. Shortly after Victoria's thirteenth birthday, her mother bought her a diary, insisting that she and Lehzen should always be able to read it. Soon after, they set out on another tour, this time around Wales.

Conroy wanted it to be as grand as possible. In her diary, Victoria wrote, "The post boys have pink silk jackets, with black hats, and the horses have pink silk reins with bunches of artificial flowers."

But Victoria was shocked by what she saw. They passed through Birmingham, then an industrial town, on their way to Wales, and Victoria had never seen such poverty before.

A Victorian painting showing a child flower-seller, forced into work by poverty

"The men, women, children, country and houses are all black… the grass is quite blasted and black…. Intermingled with wretched huts and carts and ragged little children."

As the journey went on, Victoria began to feel very unwell – sick from the constant moving around, suffering from backache and desperate to get away from the Conroys. On the afternoon of 24 September 1832, she noted in her diary that she had been, "VERY VERY VERY VERY HORRIBLY NAUGHTY!!!!", underlining each word four times.

By fourteen, Victoria was aware she was no longer a child. "I am today fourteen years old! How very old…" she wrote on her birthday. She began to feel bored in the palace, calling it 'gloomy' and 'stupid'. She studied hard, kept pet birds and played with her little spaniel, Dash, though nothing could make up for her lack of friends.

But Conroy was starting to worry. Victoria was getting older and King William IV was still in good health. He felt as if his window for power was closing. It was time for more drastic action.

Chapter 2

Fight for power

The Duchess and Conroy decided to surround Victoria with people they knew were loyal to them. Conroy's daughters became Victoria's companions, along with Lady Flora Hastings, who Victoria called the 'spy of J.C.'

Victoria, in the middle, with her mother and Conroy, far left

They also began to let it be known that the princess was weak-minded and foolish, a spoiled child, indulged by her governess, who wouldn't possibly be ready to rule at the age of eighteen.

They urged Victoria to agree that if the King died, her mother should rule as Regent until Victoria was twenty-one. At the same time, they continued to treat her like a child, teasing her that she was ugly and ignoring her if she ever complained of feeling unwell.

Victoria felt lonelier than ever, loathing her companions and believing that Lehzen was her only friend. She rebelled where she could, refusing to appoint Conroy as her adviser, however much they both might pressure her.

She was overjoyed when Feodora came for a visit, bringing her children with her. At last she had someone to confide in.

When Feodora left, Victoria wrote in her diary, "I clasped her in my arms, and kissed her and cried as if my heart would break, so did she dearest Sister..." Victoria described herself as being, "in such a state of grief that I knew not what to do with myself."

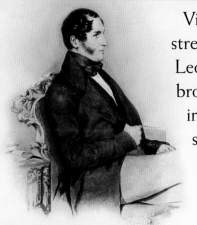

Victoria's Uncle Leopold,
King of the Belgians

Victoria tried to draw strength from her Uncle Leopold, her mother's brother, who came to visit in 1835, after Victoria's sixteenth birthday. But although Victoria called him, "the best and kindest adviser I have," he claimed he didn't like to take sides and refused to save her from the misery of Kensington Palace.

She felt weak and unwell when he left, and begged her mother to send for the doctor. At first her mother brushed away her complaints, but when Victoria's condition worsened, she at last sent an urgent summons to the doctor. He diagnosed typhoid and suggested that above all Victoria needed 'peace of mind'.

The Duchess and Conroy didn't listen, instead using Victoria's poor health to try to make Conroy her private secretary. Victoria refused, even when Conroy used threats, and his daughters and Lady Flora begged and taunted. "My beloved Lehzen supporting me alone," Victoria later wrote.

Under the strain, Victoria's hair fell out and she lost huge amounts of weight. She slowly recovered, but never forgot the way Conroy had treated her.

The following year, the seventy-year-old King became sick and weak, but he was determined to stay alive long enough to see Victoria securely on the throne. He hated the Duchess for keeping Victoria from him and setting up a rival court, and even humiliated Victoria's mother at his birthday party in front of all the guests. Embarrassed, Victoria burst into tears, and longed more than ever for independence.

As Victoria's eighteenth birthday approached, the King took a turn for the worse. "It may *all be over* at any moment and yet it *may* last a few days," Victoria wrote in her diary in May 1837. Sensing that death was near, the King wrote a letter to Victoria, promising that when she turned eighteen he would arrange for money to be given to her each year, for her use alone, with her own house and her own ladies around her. She could have full independence from her mother. Victoria was overjoyed, but her mother demanded that she refuse the offer.

They argued and Victoria went to her room, "very miserable and agitated." At last she gave in, and copied out a letter, written by her mother, claiming she was too inexperienced to accept.

Her eighteenth birthday arrived and, to the Duchess and Conroy's frustration, the King was still alive. He threw a state ball for Victoria, although he was too unwell to go to it himself.

The next day, Conroy tried to harass her into either making him her private secretary, or agreeing that she needed a regency until she was twenty-one. Lady Flora also tried to persuade Victoria on his behalf, as did Victoria's half-brother, Prince Charles of Leiningen.

Her mother desperately begged her daughter to obey Conroy. But Victoria was stronger than all of them. She was sure she was capable of ruling. She was intelligent, she could work hard and she had an ordered mind. She would not give in. Her uncle Prince Leopold sent his faithful adviser, Baron Stockmar, to help Victoria. "Whether she will hold out," Stockmar wrote, "Heaven only knows, for they plague her, every hour and every day."

As the King's health worsened, the Duchess wrote to her daughter. "You are untried, you are liked for your youth… I therefore solemnly and on my knees advise you to take Sir John Conroy." When begging failed, Conroy demanded that the Duchess use force to make her daughter obey. He told her that, "if Princess Victoria will not listen to reason, *she must be coerced.*"

In the early hours of June 20, 1837, the old King finally died. Victoria was woken by her mother at six o'clock in the morning with the news: she was finally Queen of the United Kingdom, and all the countries that made up Britain's great empire. Overnight, she had become the richest and most powerful woman in the world.

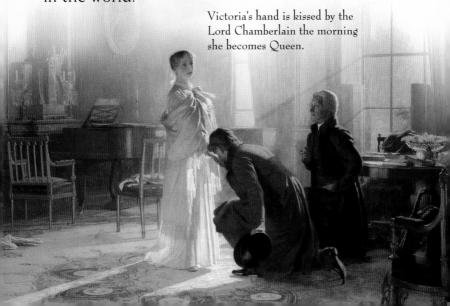

Victoria's hand is kissed by the Lord Chamberlain the morning she becomes Queen.

Queen Victoria
at eighteen, about
to ascend to the
throne

Chapter 3

The party queen

"I never was happy," Victoria later said, "until I was eighteen." Her first act as Queen was to break with her past by asking for an hour alone. She wrote short letters to her dearest relations, Leopold and Feodora, and asked that her bed be moved from her mother's room and that she have her own bedroom. She then spoke to Lord Melbourne, the Prime Minister, "of *COURSE quite ALONE*," she noted in her diary.

She liked Lord Melbourne immediately. He was fifty-eight, handsome, charming and fatherly. After her meeting with Melbourne, Victoria had to meet her Privy Councillors, two hundred and twenty of whom had gathered to see her. Lord Melbourne asked if she wished anyone to go with her, but she refused. Victoria entered the room, head held high, unafraid. Victoria was not even five feet tall, but according to one duke, "she filled the room."

The new Queen at her first Privy Council at
Kensington Palace, on 20 June, 1837

The councillors were enchanted by her
youthfulness and self-possession. As she was
leaving, however, Victoria forgot that the
Council Chamber had a glass door, and she
was seen skipping away like a schoolgirl.

She avoided her mother for the rest of
the day, before finally going down to bid her
good night. That night, for the first time in
her life, she slept alone.

For Victoria, a new life was beginning. She
had ordered Sir John Conroy's removal from
Court and she hardly saw her mother. Victoria
rose at eight each morning, worked until

breakfast, then saw her ministers between eleven and half past one. In the afternoon she went out riding with the Court.

Victoria had been isolated at Kensington, but now she was eager to learn all Lord Melbourne could teach her about politics. Years of having to live with Conroy had taught her to hide her true feelings – a useful skill as Queen. She could control her features even when her emotions were raging. Lord Melbourne was impressed but thought it "almost unnatural in one so young."

Victoria loved the "regular, hard but to me, delightful work," of a queen. She was far from beautiful, but after a succession of hoary old kings, all the old men in government were captivated by her. The public were just as enchanted. At last they had a youthful queen on the throne, bringing fresh hope for the future. At a royal event she had her hand kissed nearly three thousand times, and as her coronation day approached, eager crowds rushed to London, camping in the parks and thronging the streets.

The night before the coronation, Victoria hardly slept, feeling "that something very awful was going to happen tomorrow."

After breakfast, she dressed in robes of white satin and red velvet and left in a gilded state coach where she was cheered all the way to the Abbey. "I shall remember this day as the proudest of my life," she wrote in her diary.

As her new life took hold, Victoria sometimes felt she was living a dream. She moved from Kensington to Buckingham Palace and banished her mother to the other end of the palace. The first year of her reign was filled with excitement. She had balls and dinners, concerts and parties to go to, and everyone seemed to admire her.

But, by 1838, the constant praise was affecting her. As Stockmar wrote in one of his letters to Leopold, she was becoming, "as passionate as a

Victoria at her coronation in Westminster Abbey, surrounded by lords, ladies and bishops

spoiled child." Over-excited and over-admired, Victoria made her first mistake as Queen.

There was gossip at Court that Lady Flora Hastings, whom she had long hated, was pregnant with Sir John Conroy's child. Victoria believed the gossip and let it spread. When Lady Flora's family heard the scandal, they demanded it be investigated. Doctors came to examine Lady Flora and found that her stomach was swollen by disease. Victoria was horrified when she heard the news. She begged Lady Flora's forgiveness, but the scandal was leaked to the press and it soon became clear that Lady Flora was dying. The public began to turn against Victoria, blaming her for her cruelty and she was even hissed at while out riding.

The scandal passed and Victoria's popularity returned, but it had taken the gloss off her new life as Queen. She began to feel weary of the constant work. There were also endless political battles between the two main parties, the Whigs and the Tories, which strained her nerves. For the first time since acquiring her new-found independence, Victoria began to think about marrying.

Her thoughts turned immediately to her German cousin, Albert of Saxe-Coburg, her mother's nephew, who had visited her two years ago. On Victoria's instructions, Albert was invited over to England and arrived with his elder brother, Ernest, on 10 October, 1839. "It was with some emotion that I beheld Albert – who is *beautiful*," Victoria gushed in her diary. In less than a week, Victoria had decided that Albert was the man she wanted to marry. She wrote of his 'beautiful eyes, exquisite nose' and 'pretty mouth'. She knew he was very well read, but that he had no experience of politics or ruling. She believed she would still be in control.

As Queen, Victoria had to propose to Albert herself. "I said to him... that it would make me too happy if he would consent to what I wished... we embraced each

Albert will you marry me?

A cartoonist's impression of Victoria proposing to her cousin, Prince Albert

30

other... Oh! to *feel* I was, and am, loved by *such* an Angel as Albert."

Albert was taken aback by the almost overpowering strength of Victoria's love. But that night he handed her a note after dinner, "Dearest greatly beloved Victoria... I have to believe that Heaven has sent me an angel whose brightness shall illumine my life."

For a month, they kept their engagement a secret, only telling a select few. They basked in each other's affection. "We sit so nicely side by side on that little blue sofa; no two Lovers could ever be happier than we are!" Victoria wrote.

On 14 November, Albert's visit came to an end. Victoria was devastated by their parting. They wrote to each other constantly. Shortly afterwards, Victoria announced her engagement. But Prince Albert was not a popular choice – deemed too young, too poor, and too German.

Lord Melbourne decided the best thing would be to have a public wedding and make it something for everyone to celebrate. Victoria had wanted a small, private affair but gave in, grumbling "how everything was always made so uncomfortable for Kings and Queens."

The wedding day dawned and the heavens opened. Rain poured down but the streets were awash with well-wishers. Wearing a lace veil and a white satin gown, trimmed with orange blossom, Victoria drove through the blustery rain to the sound of cheers from the crowds. After the service in the Chapel Royal at St. James' Palace, the couple returned to Buckingham Palace for the wedding breakfast.

An oil painting of Victoria's marriage to Prince Albert, on 10 February, 1840

Guests were amazed at the huge cake, so heavy it took four men to carry it in. Then the royal couple left for their honeymoon at Windsor Castle. Houses all along the route were lit up with crowns and stars.

Albert had wanted to spend four or six weeks away, but Victoria had insisted that was too long. She told her husband she needed to be in London for work and that a few days would have to do. "Your forget, my dearest love, that I am the Sovereign." She was in love with Albert, but she was also in love with power.

Chapter 4

Wife and mother

At the start of her married life, Victoria clung to her independence. She told Prince Albert that, "the English are very jealous of any foreigner intefering in the government of this country." They soon began to argue. Victoria did not want to talk politics with Albert; he insisted on it. Victoria wanted no more than loyal support from Albert, while he desperately wanted an active role in running the country.

Then, shortly after their honeymoon, Victoria discovered she was pregnant. "I must say that... I am really upset about it and it is spoiling my happiness; I have always hated the idea..." Victoria even told her Uncle Leopold that if she only produced a 'nasty girl' at the end of it, she would drown her. She wanted a son and heir for the country, but nine months after her wedding day, Victoria gave birth to a healthy baby girl, christened Victoria after her mother, though she would always be known as Vicky.

Despite her fears, Victoria was soon delighted by her baby, more and more so as she grew older. She was not, however, a doting mother, only seeing her baby twice a day, and referring to her as 'the Child'.

Queen Victoria with the Princess Royal

But however much Victoria disliked the idea, the birth of her baby had forever shifted the balance of power between her and Albert. On the day the Princess Royal was born, Albert represented Victoria at the Privy Council for the first time. Two weeks later, as Victoria lay recovering, she gave him the key to her confidential boxes, with all the details of secret government discussions. The following year, Albert was being sent the latest news from the Foreign Office. With Victoria now busy in her role as mother, Albert had grasped some of her power. Their partnership had begun.

When Lord Melbourne was defeated in the election of 1841, and a new Prime Minister took over, Prince Albert stepped in as her closest advisor. From then on, she began to lean on him 'for all and everything', describing him as her 'Lord and Master'.

Their writing desks at Buckingham Palace were placed side by side, to help them work together and they fell into an easy routine, working separately in the morning, then meeting to discuss business before lunch. In the afternoon they usually saw ministers together, then went riding. Dinner was at eight, and Albert tried to

A portrait of family life at Windsor Castle, with the Princess Royal in the corner

insist on only very serious conversations. He heavily disapproved of any flirting or gossiping at Court. Victoria's early love of gaiety and parties was being slowly drowned out by Albert's more serious approach to life.

The only thorn between them now was Lehzen, Victoria's old governess, who ruled over Buckingham Palace. Victoria was forever grateful to Lehzen for having supported her in her battles with Conroy. Albert called her the 'House Dragon' for her intefering ways. Not understanding the extent of Victoria's unhappiness in childhood, and how much Lehzen had helped her, he just wished to be rid of her.

The Queen still struggled with her temper, picking fights with Albert whenever she felt low, then flying into rages when they argued. Afterwards, she was always filled with remorse. "I will strive to conquer it though I knew before I married that this would be a trouble..."

For two and half years before her marriage she had been her own mistress. Now she found it hard to bend to another's will. But her love for Albert won out.

"I am ready to submit to his wishes as I love him so dearly," she wrote in 1842. In September that year, Lehzen was quietly persuaded to retire.

In total, the Queen had nine children, seven of whom were born in the first ten years of their marriage. Victoria spent most of the 1840s either pregnant or in the nursery. She gave birth to a boy, Bertie, the year after the Princess Royal, swiftly followed by Alice in 1843, Alfred in 1844, Helena in 1846, Louise in 1848 and Arthur in 1850. Leopold, the last boy, was born in 1853 and then Beatrice, always known as 'Baby', in 1857. Though the Queen claimed she disliked babies, especially "their big body and little limbs and that terrible frog-like action," she became much fonder of her children as they grew up.

Lehzen's departure also finally paved the way for Victoria to make up with her mother. Albert acted as peacemaker, until Victoria found that, "Every succeeding year seemed to draw beloved Mama nearer and nearer to me." Their shared love of Victoria's children acted as a strong bond between them, and Victoria increasingly turned to her mother for help and advice.

By 1843, Victoria had decided she wanted 'a place of their own', where they could spend private time as a family. She was partly driven by the fear that the Court might spoil and corrupt her children. Two years later, they bought Osborne House on the Isle of Wight, which Prince Albert helped redesign, attempting to recreate for his children the magic of his own childhood. "How happy we are here!" the Queen wrote in July 1849. "And never do I enjoy myself more... than when I can be so much with my beloved Albert and follow him everywhere."

A sketch, done in 1850, by Queen Victoria herself, of her children in the gardens at Osborne House, on the Isle of Wight

The Queen adored their new home, and wanted to buy another in Scotland. She had fallen in love with the Highlands, with the solitude and amazing views of mountains and lochs. In 1848, they bought Balmoral Castle and were soon learning Scottish reels, wearing kilts and taking long walks around the lochs. "It was wonderful," wrote the Queen, "not seeing a single human being, nor hearing a sound excepting that of the wind, or the call of the blackcock or grouse."

This is a view of Balmoral Castle in 1880. The original castle was demolished and a new one built to Prince Albert's designs.

Their escapes to Osborne and Balmoral fulfilled Victoria and Albert's desire that their children, "should be brought up as simply, and in as domestic a way as possible." Meals were plain, clothes were passed down and both parents spent a lot of time with their children.

"Come along my chicks," Queen Victoria would call, taking her children out into the garden. Prince Albert, so stiff and formal in company, was at his most relaxed with his children, playing hide and seek, flying kites or chasing butterflies with them.

In 1848 a series of revolutions ripped across Europe, toppling royal families from their thrones. Buckingham Palace was soon filled with royal refugees. The events enforced Victoria's belief that, "we are before God all alike and that in the twinkling of an eye - the highest may find themselves at the feet of the poorest and the lowest." She wanted her children to see this at first hand, so she took them on visits to the poor around Balmoral and tried to teach them to be humble and to do 'good works' for others.

Some of her children recalled their childhood as blissful. "What a joyous childhood we had," Alice later told her mother, but others felt they suffered under her controlling love. Leopold, her fifth son, had a disease which meant he was in constant danger of bleeding to death. Victoria became so over-protective that Leopold ended up rebelling.

Some of her children resented Victoria and Albert's attempts to force them to follow their ideals. Louise later recalled her parents' terrible "habit of moulding all children to the same pattern," while Bertie, the heir to the throne, was made to feel a disappointment for not being more like his father. His parents complained constantly about his laziness and idleness until he felt he could never do right.

Victoria's love was so possessive, and in some cases selfish, she found it hard to part from her daughters when they married. She told Vicky, her eldest, how awful she found it – "she is gone, as your own child, for ever; she belongs to another..." She was also horrified when she discovered that Beatrice, her youngest, was in love, and for a while even refused to let her be married.

All nine of Queen Victoria's children, in 1865 (from left): Leopold, Louise, Beatrice, Alice, Bertie, Arthur, Vicky, Alfred and Helena

Victoria adored her children, but her love for them always came second to her love for Albert. "*ALL* the numerous children are as *nothing* to me when *he is away*," she wrote to her Uncle Leopold. "It seems as if the whole life of the house and home are gone..."

Her pride in him was full to overflowing after he arranged the Great Exhibition of 1851. Held inside the Crystal Palace, a huge building made of glass and iron, it celebrated Britain's industry and empire. Millions of people from all over the

Here you can see the building that housed the Great Exhibition. It was a massive glass structure with a cast iron frame.

world visited the Exhibition to see printing presses, steam engines, Russian furs, Tunisian tents and much, much more. Prince Albert used the money raised to set up free museums and art galleries in London.

Despite all his hard work, Albert remained unpopular with the public. But Victoria's love for him never dimmed. She claimed she always felt, "the same tender love" for him as she did in, "the *very first days of our marriage!*"

She listened to Albert and was guided by him. For his sake, she tried to curb her temper and her diary was crowded with resolutions to mend her ways, "to become worthier, less full of weakness and failings." "Self is still far too prominent!" she wrote. "I must crush it!"

She also followed his lead in trying to rise above party politics and to give the monarchy a more caring role, by showing concern for the hardships of working people. But while Prince Albert worked tirelessly to improve working people's lives, the Queen was afraid of any rapid change to the structure of society.

Albert was the more practical one, but it was Victoria who felt a deeply personal relationship with her subjects. When the Crimean War broke out in 1854, Victoria was proud to speak of the soliders as 'her own' and even as her 'children'. Once the wounded began returning to England, she spent much of her time visiting them. She bought wooden limbs for those who couldn't afford them and used her influence to find jobs for the disabled.

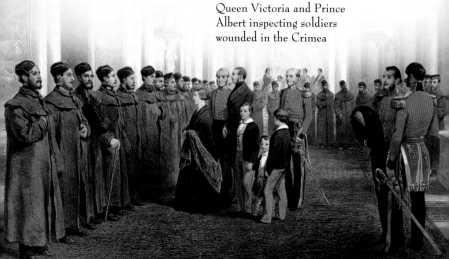

Queen Victoria and Prince Albert inspecting soldiers wounded in the Crimea

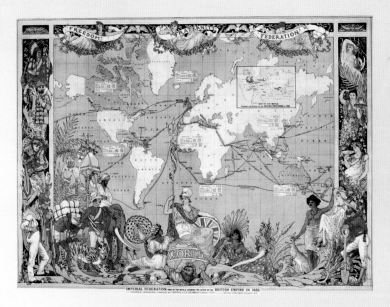

This is a map of the world as it was in Queen Victoria's time. All the areas ruled by the British Empire have been shaded.

Victoria extended that personal relationship to the people of India when it became part of the British empire in 1858. She insisted that the Proclamation of British rule be rewritten, wanting it to "breathe feelings of generosity, benevolence..." and made sure it promised to respect India's native religions and would not try to change them. She said she felt a deep sense of pride, "to feel herself in direct communication," with the people of India.

Victoria drew much of her strength from Albert. "Truly," she wrote later, "he was my entire self, my very life and soul... Surely there can never again be such a union, such trust and understanding between two people."

In March 1861, she needed him more than ever, when she discovered her mother was dying. "I knelt before her," she wrote in her diary, "kissed her dear hand and placed it next to my cheek..." That night she slept fitfully on the sofa and watched the next morning as her mother's life finally ebbed away.

Queen Victoria and Prince Albert together, in 1852

For the next six months, the Queen was inconsolable. She lost her appetite and suffered constant headaches, her grief intensified by guilt at all the years of estrangement. To try to cheer her up, Prince Albert took her to Scotland. One of the Queen's companions spoke of Albert's "gentleness" and "tenderness... Oh! he is one in millions - well might She love Him as She did."

The Queen gradually recovered, but worse was to come. In December that year, Prince Albert became unwell. For three days he refused all food, and wandered restlessly from room to room or lay in bed. A few days later a rash appeared. "I went to my room," wrote the Queen, "and cried dreadfully and felt oh! as if my heart must break."

The doctor diagnosed typhoid. Over the next few days the prince sometimes seemed better. One evening he stroked the Queen's cheek and called her *Liebes Frauchen*, "Dear little wife," but at other times his mind wandered. The Queen stayed by his side, managing to seem cheerful. As he drew his last breath, the Queen clutched his cold hand. "Oh, yes, this is death," she said. Then she cried out "Oh! My dear Darling!" and sank to her knees in despair.

Chapter 5

The woman in black

The Queen declared that the moment Prince Albert died she was, "changed from a powerful sovereign... into a weak and desolate woman." She would go to sleep each night clutching 'his dear red dressing-gown'. "There is no one left to hold me in their arms and press me to their heart," she wrote. From the time of his death, she dressed only in black.

The Queen moved to Osborne House and began refusing to see her ministers. When she had to hold a Privy Council, she listened to the meeting through a half-open door, while the ministers had to shout at the top of their voices so she could hear them in the next room.

Her daughter, Princess Alice, tried to comfort her. "How you suffered was dreadful to witness," she told her mother later, "it tore my heart to pieces."

The greatest comfort Victoria found was at Balmoral. "The mountains, the woods, the rocks seem to talk of him, for he wandered and climbed so often among them," she told the Queen of Prussia. Victoria clung to grief and refused to let it go. She still read state papers and was kept informed of all that went on, but she refused to attend any official events, including the opening of Parliament.

The Queen at Balmoral in 1863 with two of her daughters, in front of a portrait of Prince Albert

At first, the public was understanding, but after two years the people demanded her return. Their Queen was not only spending up to five months of the year in Scotland, but she had also become invisible. Someone even put a sign on the railings outside Buckingham Palace which said 'to let or be sold'.

This is the Albert Memorial, in Kensington Gardens. It was commissioned by Queen Victoria and took ten years to complete.

Ministers, courtiers and her own children tried to coax her out of her retirement, but she was too stubborn to respond.

She tried to keep everything as Albert had left it. His coat still hung in the hall at Osborne House; his desk remained untouched. Every day his clothes were laid out on his chair and his soap and towels were replaced.

The Queen turned away from society, and instead she formed close friendships with some of the humblest of her subjects. One of them was John Brown, a servant at Balmoral, who had been ordered to take the Queen out riding to improve her health. The Queen liked his blunt, plain-spoken ways and felt at ease with him. They became devoted to each other, but their friendship caused a scandal at Court, and then among the people. Gossips hinted that they had secretly married and some people nicknamed her 'Mrs. Brown', but those closest to her insisted on her innocence.

An oil painting, commissioned by the Queen, showing her on horseback with John Brown

The Queen also relied more than ever on her daughters. Alice slept in her mother's room every night and, when she married, her younger sister Helena took her place as her mother's chief carer. When it was Helena's turn to marry, she moved nearby and the lot of companion then fell to Beatrice, the youngest.

Eventually, the Queen had to respond to the growing demand for her to take up her public duties. In June 1864, she appeared again on the streets of London in an open carriage, which she found '*very painful,*' although she was cheered by the warmth of the public's greeting. In 1866 she was even persuaded to open Parliament, although the experience left her shaken and exhausted. But her appearances were too few and far between.

Queen Victoria visiting Victoria Park, London, in an open carriage, with well-wishers lining her path

People complained about her constant demands for money for her children and began suggesting the country might be better off with no royal family at all.

Then, in 1871, Bertie caught typhoid. The Queen sat by his bed holding 'his poor hand' and dreading the worst, but Bertie

Bertie, Prince of Wales, photographed in 1870

slowly recovered. The Queen was incredibly touched by the feeling shown by the people. After a thanksgiving service, she appeared several times on the balcony at Buckingham Palace, waving to the cheering crowds. The tide had turned. Those who were speaking out against the monarchy found people had started to love the royal family again. And Victoria, moved by their affection, began to take up her public role of Queen once more.

Queen Victoria in 1886, wearing
her small diamond crown

Chapter 6

Grandmother of Europe

In the 1870s, Queen Victoria began to feel a new zest for life. In part this was due to Benjamin Disraeli, her new Prime Minister. He had a magical gift for words, which he used to turn Victoria from a recluse into one of the best-loved queens in history. "Everyone likes flattery," he once remarked, "and when you come to royalty you should lay it on with a trowel."

Instead of trying to force the Queen to appear in public, he built up her confidence. He made her feel as if they were running the country together, asking her advice on political matters, referring to her, "almost unrivalled experience."

In 1876, Disraeli persuaded the Queen to take on the new title Empress of India, describing India as the 'jewel' in her crown. The Queen took her new role seriously.

She surrounded herself with Indians at Court, was quick to point out they should be treated as equals and thought any prejudice 'reprehensible.' She even began to learn Hindustani, one of the languages spoken in India.

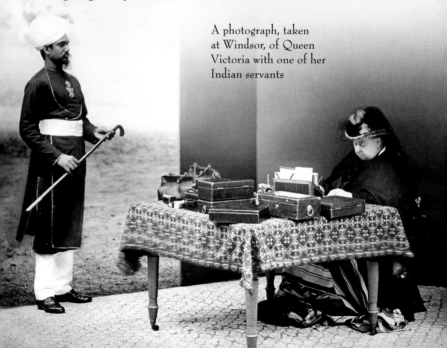

A photograph, taken at Windsor, of Queen Victoria with one of her Indian servants

When not on her travels or busying herself with politics, the Queen was setting herself up as the matchmaker of Europe. She took her role as head of the family as seriously as that of Head of State. She involved herself not only in the lives and marriages of her children, but in those of her grandchildren too.

When her daughter Alice died, she took charge of her children, calling them, "doubly dear as the children of my *own* darling child I have lost and loved so much."

One grandaughter described her as, "the central power directing things," whose, "*yes* or *no* counted tremendously." She frequently had her grandchildren to stay, even allowing them to play around her feet as she worked.

Victoria wanted her descendents to be able to marry for love, as well as position. When one of her grandaughters chose to marry a lesser royal, the family were horrified by the match. But Victoria wrote, "I think you have done very well to choose only a husband who is *quite* of your way of thinking." He wasn't wealthy but, she said, "I don't think riches make happiness."

As a result of her matchmaking, Victoria's children and grandchildren were to sit on the thrones of Russia, Norway, Germany, Greece, Denmark, Romania, Sweden and Spain. Victoria's involvement in their lives went so far that she even insisted her grandchildren used English nannies to bring up their children.

The Queen with her great-grandchildren in 1899. From left: the future George VI, Princess Mary, the future Edward VIII and Henry, later Duke of Gloucester.

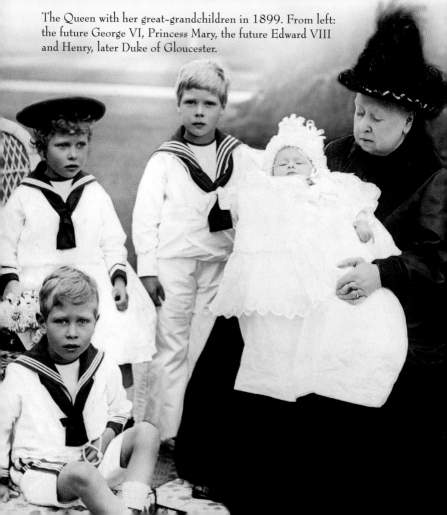

In June 1887, the Queen celebrated her Golden Jubilee, to mark her fifty years on the the throne. She drove through the streets in an open carriage, but refused to wear a crown or dress in royal robes. She was escorted by four kings and surrounded by princes. Millions of people crowded onto the streets. The day was described by an observer as, "one continuous roar of cheering." One of the photographs taken of her was so unflattering that her daughters wanted it banned, but the Queen was completely without vanity. "I have *no* illusions," she said, "about my personal appearance."

This painting shows a garden party at Buckingham Palace, celebrating the Queen's Diamond Jubilee, in 1897. The Queen, and her daughter-in-law, are in the carriage.

The older the Queen grew, the more she seemed to enjoy life. Every afternoon she went out in her carriage for a drive, whatever the weather, amazing everyone that she never caught a cold. On her eightieth birthday she declared that she was never in, "better health or higher spirits." Two years earlier, she had

Queen Victoria, smiling as she rides in an open carriage, in 1893

celebrated her Diamond Jubilee, proudly noting in her diary that, "Today is the day on which I have reigned longer, by a day, than any English Sovereign." She was so touched by the warmth of the public, that tears ran down her cheeks. "How kind they are!" she kept saying.

Towards the end of her life, the Queen was struck with rheumatism and could only walk with the help of a stick, but she always made light of it. She also began to lose her sight, relying on Princess Beatrice for help with reading and writing.

By February 1900, Victoria's strength had started to fail. "I now rest daily," she noted in her diary. By October she was much thinner and her spirits had left her. She apologized to her eldest daughter for being, "a poor old thing not almost myself."

Her health was also affected by her worry over the war the British were fighting in South Africa, and she could no longer sleep at night. Her opening entry in her diary in January 1901 reads, "Another year begun and I am feeling so weak and unwell that I enter upon it sadly." By 22 January, at the grand old age of eighty-one, the Queen woke to her last morning. She called for her son, Bertie, by name, and died with her family around her, in the arms of her eldest grandson.

Queen Victoria's funeral procession, passing Marble Arch, on 2 February, 1901

Epilogue

Victoria had spent her last 40 years in black, but she ordered a white funeral. Her coffin was covered in white flowers and was carried to Windsor, where she was buried beside Albert. "What a Queen she was," wrote her eldest daughter, "and what a woman."

The Queen was head of the European royal family, the longest reigning monarch and ruler of the greatest empire. For many who stood on the streets that day to watch her coffin go past, she had seemed a permanent fixture in their lives. It was almost impossible to imagine England without her. The Queen Empress had come a long way from the stubborn little girl at Kensington who refused to play the piano.

Victoria and Albert's tomb at the Frogmore Mausoleum, Windsor

ACKNOWLEDGEMENTS

© akg-images p13 (IAM), p14; © Bridgeman Art Library p1 (FORBES Magazine Collection, New York, USA), p3 (Guildhall Library, City of London), p16 (Art Gallery of South Australia, Adelaide, Australia/Gift of Charles Drew 1889), p18 (British Library Board. All Rights Reserved), p23 (2011 Her Majesty Queen Elizabeth II), p26 (2011 Her Majesty Queen Elizabeth II), p28 (Bradford Art Galleries and Museums, West Yorkshire, UK), p30tr (Ashmolean Museum, University of Oxford, UK), pp32-3 (2011 Her Majesty Queen Elizabeth II), p35 (Christopher Wood Gallery, London, UK), p36 (2011 Her Majesty Queen Elizabeth II), p39 (2011 Her Majesty Queen Elizabeth II), p44-5 (The Stapleton Collection), p46 (National Army Museum, London), p47 (Royal Geographical Society, London, UK), p53 (FORBES Magazine Collection, New York, USA), p60 (2011 Her Majesty Queen Elizabeth II), p62 (Private Collection); © Corbis spine (Gianni Dagli Orti), p7 (Stapleton Collection), p10 (Michael Freeman), p30bl (Bettmann), p48 (Bettmann), p52 (Rudy Sulgan), p56 (Gianni Dagli Orti), p57 (Derek Bayes/Lebrecht Music & A/Lebrecht Music & Arts), p59 (Bettmann), p61; © Getty Images cover (SuperStock), p8, p20, p24 (SuperStock), p51, p55; © Mary Evans Picture Library p5, p6, p40-1, p43 (Charlotte Zeepvat/ILN), p54 (Illustrated London News Ltd), p63 (Sueddeutsche Zeitung Photo).

Please note some of the black and white images in the
book have been digitally tinted by Usborne.

Internet links

You can find out more about Queen Victoria by
going to the Usborne Quicklinks website at
www.usborne-quicklinks.com
and typing the keywords "queen victoria".

Edited by Jane Chisholm

Digital manipulation by Keith Furnival

First published in 2012 by Usborne Publishing Ltd., Usborne House, 83-85 Saffron Hill, London EC1N 8RT, England. www.usborne.com Copyright © 2012 Usborne Publishing Ltd.